Future Tech

The Future of
Medicine

Kevin Kurtz

Lerner Publications ◆ Minneapolis

Lerner Publications Company
An imprint of Lerner Publishing Group, Inc.
241 First Avenue North
Minneapolis, MN 55401 USA

For reading levels and more information, look up this title at www.lernerbooks.com.

Main body text set in Adrianna Regular.
Typeface provided by Chank.

Editor: Rebecca Higgins **Designer**: Amy Salveson **Photo Editor**: Rebecca Higgins

Library of Congress Cataloging-in-Publication Data

Names: Kurtz, Kevin, author.
Title: The future of medicine / Kevin Kurtz.
Description: Minneapolis : Lerner Publications, [2021] | Series: Searchlight books.
    Future tech | Includes bibliographical references and index. | Audience: Ages 8–11. |
    Audience: Grades 2–3. | Summary: "Doctors work hard to help people who are sick,
    but what if you never got sick? Explore the future of medicine, from watches that
    track your body's processes to gene editing"— Provided by publisher.
Identifiers: LCCN 2019049873 (print) | LCCN 2019049874
(ebook) | ISBN 9781541597358 (library binding) | ISBN 9781728413822 (paperback) |
    ISBN 9781728400839 (ebook)
Subjects: LCSH: Medicine—Forecasting—Juvenile literature. | Medical innovations—
    Juvenile literature. | Medical technology—Juvenile literature. | Medical care—
    Utilization—Juvenile literature.
Classification: LCC R130.5 .K87 2021 (print) | LCC R130.5 (ebook) | DDC 610—dc23

LC record available at https://lccn.loc.gov/2019049873
LC ebook record available at https://lccn.loc.gov/2019049874

Manufactured in the United States of America
1-47839-48279-2/12/2020

Contents

Chapter 1

A HEALTHIER FUTURE

Imagine you are going to the doctor in the 1860s. You would have a very different experience than the one you would have today. You tell the nineteenth-century doctor you have a bad headache. He treats it by sticking a bloodsucking leech onto your skin. Or maybe you see the doctor because you have an infection in your hand. He tells you the only way to stop the infection is to cut off your arm.

A doctor places a leech on a patient's foot.

Modern medicine has helped people live longer.

Medicine has come a long way. In the nineteenth century, most people did not live into their fifties. Today, many people in the United States live into their eighties or nineties. Doctors know more about what causes illness in our bodies and are better equipped to treat medical issues.

While modern medicine allows doctors to do amazing things, there is still a lot they don't know. For example, doctors don't know how to fight aggressive cancers without creating harmful side effects. The practice of medicine still has a lot of room for improvement.

Scientists are researching better ways to fight cancer.

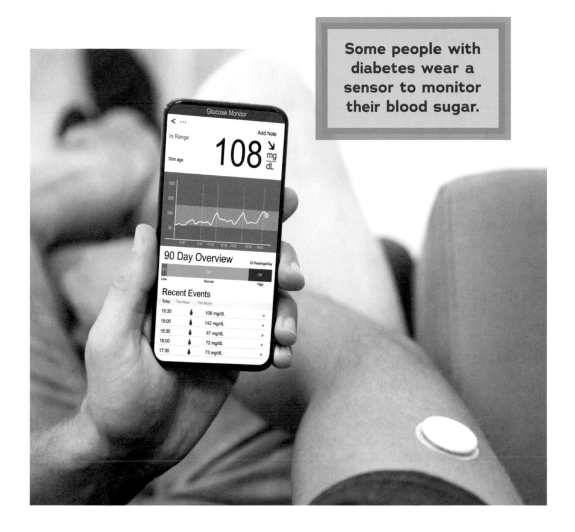

A Glimpse at Tomorrow

New medical technologies are on their way. In the future, doctors may operate on you without cutting your skin. You may receive vaccines painlessly by wearing a patch. If you need a new kidney, you could get one 3D printed specially for you. The future of medicine promises to make us healthier.

Chapter 2

A BULL'S-EYE ON CANCER

Doctors treat cancer in many ways. Radiation therapy blasts a cancerous tumor with X-rays or other types of radiation. Chemotherapy puts chemicals that attack cancer into the body. But these treatments don't just attack cancer cells. They also attack healthy cells. When healthy cells are attacked, patients can experience negative side effects such as hair loss, vomiting, and pain.

Chemotherapy damages cancer cells and healthy cells.

HEALTHY WHITE BLOOD CELLS SURROUND AND ATTACK A CANCER CELL.

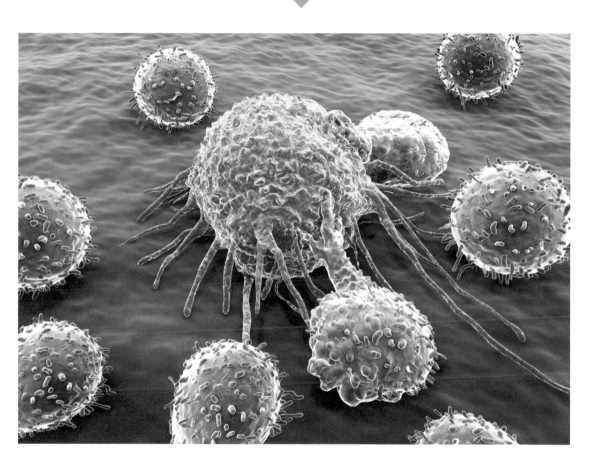

Scientists are working on cancer treatments that target only cancer cells. Healthy cells are left alone. These targeted treatments prevent patients from feeling even sicker.

Enlisting the Immune System

Our bodies have a natural defense against disease. The immune system finds and kills germs, the microbes that cause illness. This prevents us from getting sick. But the immune system does not realize cancer cells are dangerous, so it doesn't fight them.

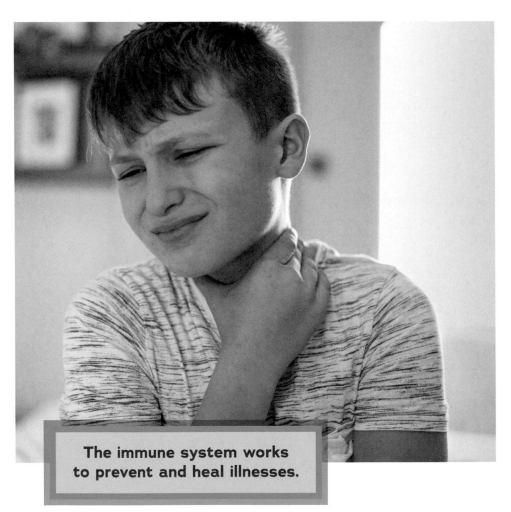

The immune system works to prevent and heal illnesses.

Vaccines prevent
diseases caused by
viruses and bacteria.

Scientists are figuring out ways to train the immune
system to fight cancer. One way might be a cancer
vaccine. Vaccines introduce tiny amounts of weakened
bacteria or viruses into your body so your immune
system can recognize the germs and fight them. The
cancer vaccine would inject cancer cells. Then the
immune system could learn to seek and destroy cancer
in the body.

Special Delivery

Bacteria might also be able to fight cancer. Genes tell a cell what to do. By changing bacteria's genes, scientists could reprogram bacteria to find cancer in the body. The bacteria would create antibodies that could invade the cancer cells and kill them. Scientists could program the bacteria to self-destruct once the cancer is destroyed.

ANTIBODIES ATTACK VIRUSES.

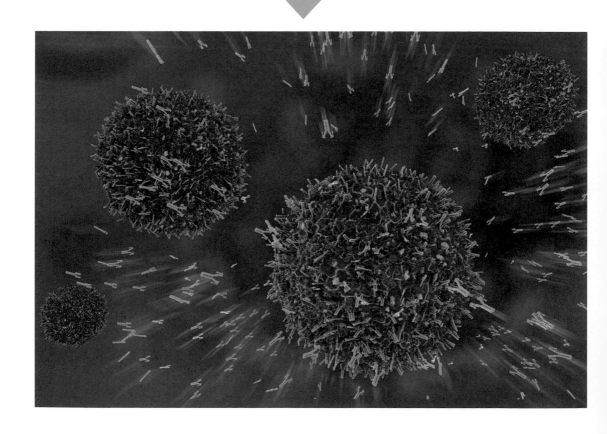

Another way to stop cancer is through surgery. Unfortunately, surgery can damage organs near cancer tumors. To prevent this, future surgery may be done by robots. Robot surgeons do not have shaky hands. They can reach smaller spaces in the body than human hands can. A robot surgeon would operate while imaging machines look into the body. The machines would give the robot a 3D view of the tumor. The robot could make sure each cut is in the right place.

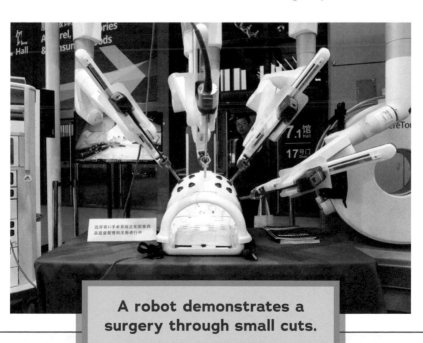

A robot demonstrates a surgery through small cuts.

Chapter 3

TRILLIONS OF HEALTH ALLIES

For much of human history, no one knew why people got sick. Then, in the middle of the nineteenth century, scientists such as John Snow and Louis Pasteur made a major discovery. They proved that some diseases are caused by microbes. This breakthrough saved millions of lives. Doctors knew to target microbes to stop diseases from spreading. But the discovery also led many people to assume all microbes were harmful. People have been trying to kill all the microbes they could ever since.

Louis Pasteur is known for his work on microbes and the food-preserving process, pasteurization.

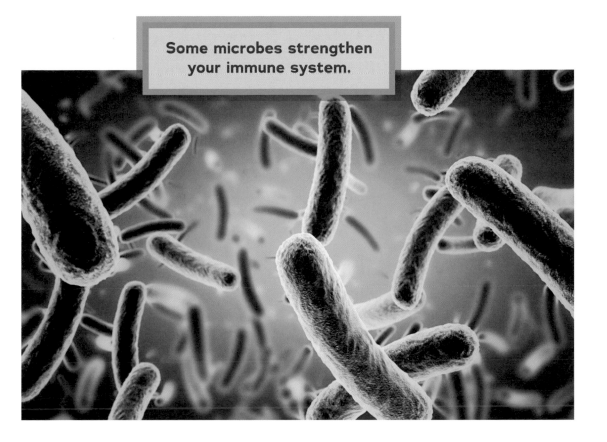

Some microbes strengthen your immune system.

New research is showing that this is a mistake. Scientists are finding that less than 1 percent of bacterial species cause harm. Trillions of microbes that are necessary for our health live inside and on our bodies. These microbes turn the food we eat into nutrients our bodies can use. They prevent dangerous microbes from infecting our bodies. Evidence even shows that microbes in our guts send signals to our brains and that those signals affect how we feel.

Allergies, asthma, and autoimmune diseases can be caused by the immune system attacking something harmless. The rise in these conditions seems to be happening because many people do not have the right microbes in their bodies. Overuse of antibiotics and certain foods in modern diets remove the body's good microbes. Without the right microbes, the immune system can end up hurting itself.

OVERUSE OF ANTIBIOTICS MAKES BACTERIA HARDER TO TREAT.

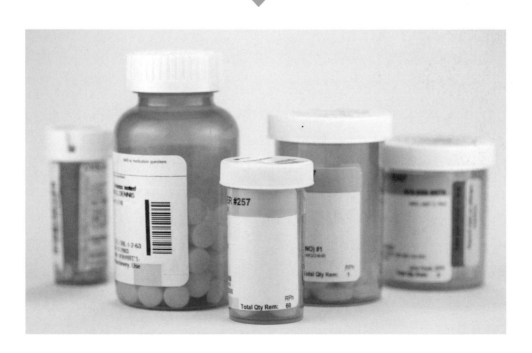

A doctor studies microbes.

Trillions of microbes live inside and on our bodies. A microbiome is a group of microbes that live together. In the future, doctors will pay close attention to the microbe species in our microbiomes. They will make sure we have the right microbe species to keep us healthy.

The Future of Ew!

It's easy to see if you have the right microbes living in your gut. Just look at your poop. Between 25 and 54 percent of poop is made of gut microbes. If your poop shows you have the wrong microbes, doctors may give you someone else's poop. This is called a fecal transplant. The poop comes from a donor with a healthy microbiome. Once the donor's poop is inside you, the right microbes multiply in your gut to keep you healthy.

There are thousands of different types of microbes in your gut.

A Parasite Prescription

To stay healthy, we need microbes living inside us, but we may also need worms. Roundworms inside a person's gut have been shown to cure hay fever. Whipworms can prevent inflammatory bowel syndrome. Parasitic worms have lived inside people for tens of thousands of years. The human body evolved to work with the worms. In the future, you may be prescribed live intestinal worms to treat certain diseases.

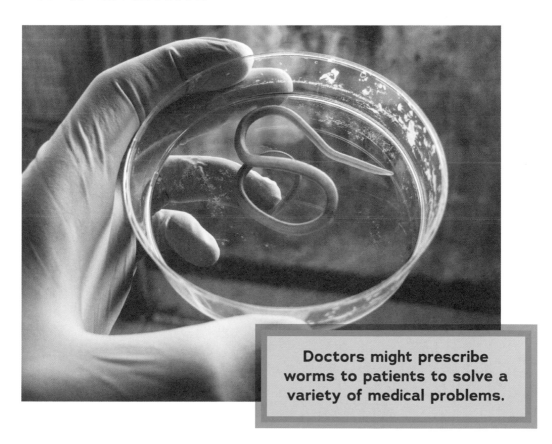

Doctors might prescribe worms to patients to solve a variety of medical problems.

Chapter 4

MEDICINE JUST FOR YOU

Modern medical care is based on how most people's bodies react to treatments. But what if your body reacts differently? You could be stuck with treatment that doesn't work for you. You might even experience dangerous side effects.

The wrong treatment could mean being sick longer.

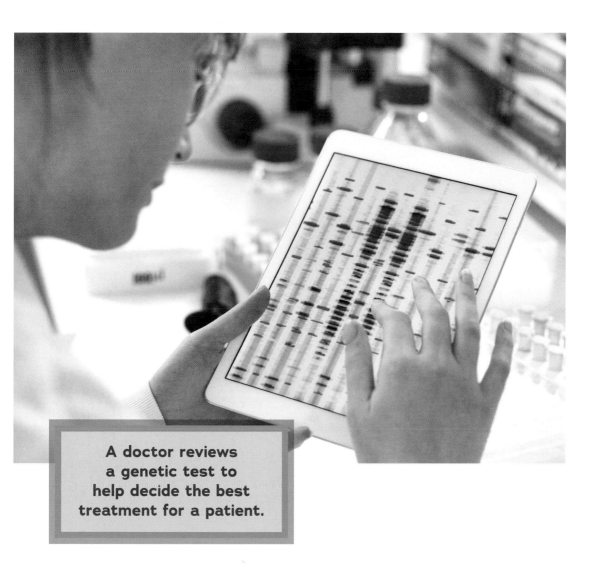

**A doctor reviews
a genetic test to
help decide the best
treatment for a patient.**

In the future, doctors will pay more attention to your
body's unique characteristics. They will look at traits
such as your genes, microbiome, and eating and sleeping
habits. They will determine which treatments will work
best for your body. This is called precision medicine.

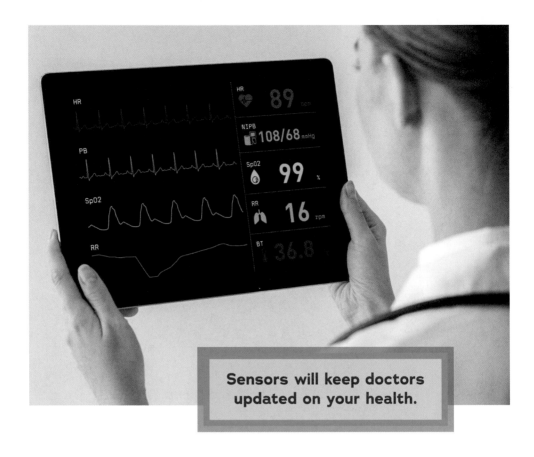

Sensors will keep doctors updated on your health.

For precision medicine to work, doctors will need a lot of data on each person. The data helps them to understand how each person's body normally behaves and how it reacts to medical treatments. People will need to get more physicals and medical tests. We might wear sensors, such as smartwatches, to collect more data on our bodies. This daily data will help doctors to discover when something unusual is happening in your body. Doctors could treat health issues before they become serious problems.

Modified Babies

Everyone has different genes. Some genes cause illnesses such as cystic fibrosis or hemophilia. In the future, doctors could remove these genes before a baby is even born. That way, the baby might never get the illness.

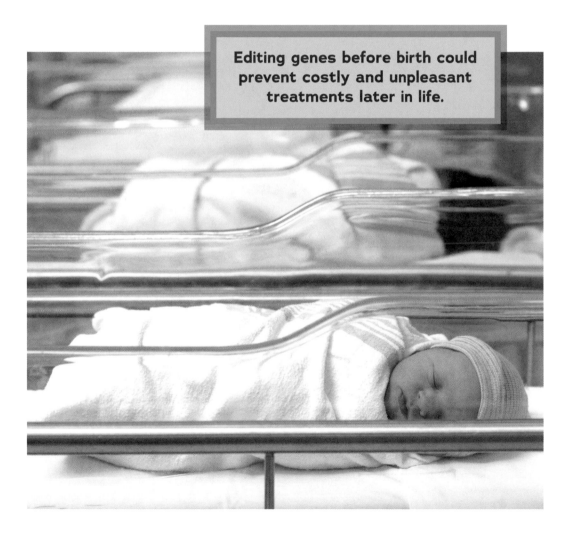

Editing genes before birth could prevent costly and unpleasant treatments later in life.

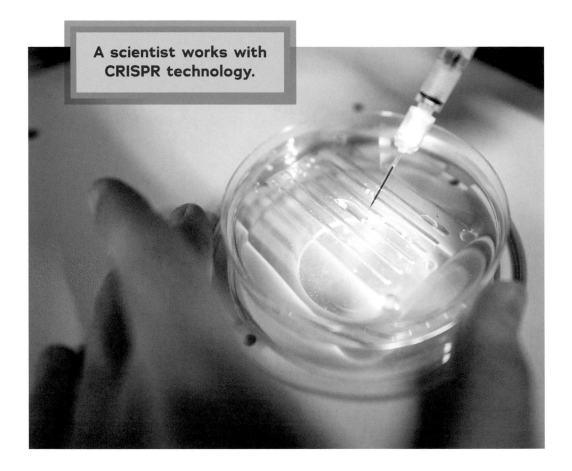

A scientist works with CRISPR technology.

A new technology called CRISPR allows scientists to swap out genes in cells. CRISPR could remove the genes that cause illnesses and disorders.

Some people are concerned about this technology. Experts are still learning all the things our genes do. It's possible that illness-causing genes also do other things in the body. Removing these genes might hurt a person in unexpected ways.

Another concern is that only wealthy people would be able to afford this treatment. Rich parents could edit their babies' genes to make them superkids. Meanwhile, other parents would leave their children's genetic issues unfixed. Tailored genes could give children from wealthy families unfair advantages.

SUPERKIDS COULD BE HEALTHIER THAN OTHER KIDS.

Custom Kidneys

People with kidney failure need a kidney transplant. They have to wait for someone to donate a kidney. Unfortunately, the demand for healthy kidneys is much greater than the supply. And the donated kidney has to be the right match for the patient. For example, if the donated kidney does not have a compatible blood type, the patient's body will reject it. On average, people wait about three years for a kidney transplant. Every day, about thirteen people die waiting for a kidney.

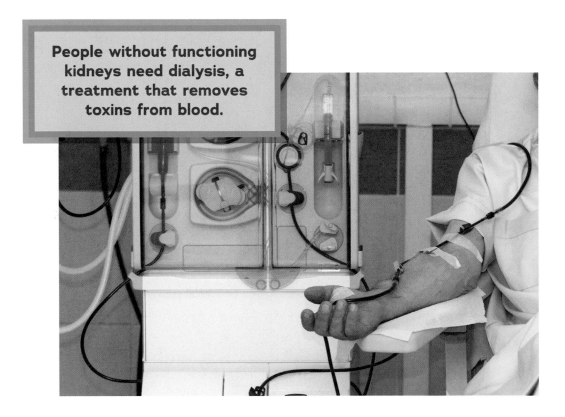

People without functioning kidneys need dialysis, a treatment that removes toxins from blood.

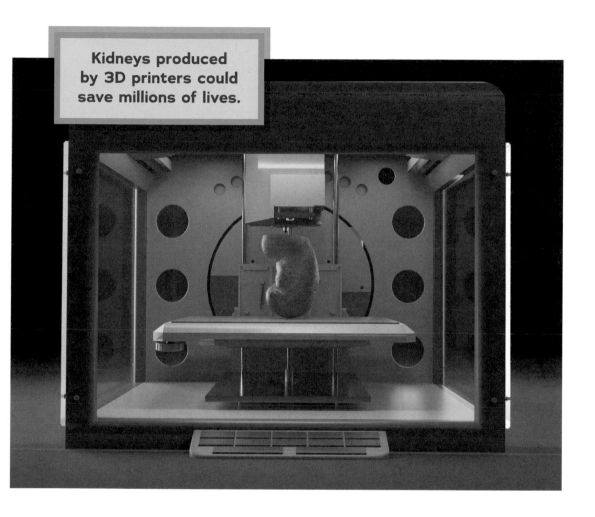

Kidneys produced by 3D printers could save millions of lives.

In the future, patients may not need to wait for a donor. Doctors could 3D print a replacement kidney. They would take healthy cells from the patient's body and use them to grow more cells in a lab. They would then print the kidney using these living cells. The printed kidney is already alive, functioning, and compatible with the patient's body. This will allow people to get kidneys when they need them, saving many lives.

STEM Spotlight

Many medical treatments involve jabbing sharp metal objects into our bodies. This may change in the future. Ultrasound is an energy wave that can pass through bodies harmlessly. When the wave reaches the right spot, a surgeon can direct it to heat up. This pinpointed heat could perform operations without cutting the skin.

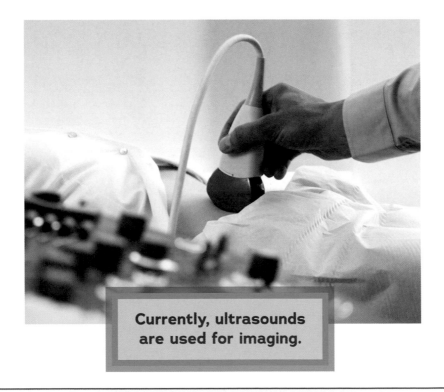

Currently, ultrasounds are used for imaging.

The Future Is Never Certain

We do not know for sure that these new treatments will come into use. The human body is very complex. Doctors have much more to learn about our health. Though some of these treatments might not work, research and innovation will continue. Medicine will become more effective and focused on our needs, building us a healthier future.

Scientists are researching new ways to keep people healthy.

Glossary

antibiotic: a medicine that kills bacteria in the body to stop diseases and infections

antibody: a substance made by a living thing to kill germs and other infecting cells

chemotherapy: using chemicals to treat diseases, such as cancer

gene: the part of a cell that tells the cell how to grow and what to do

imaging: using technology to create a 3D image of the inside of the body

immune system: the body's system that protects it from germs that cause diseases

microbe: a living thing that has only one cell

microbiome: all the microbes that live inside and on a body

sensor: a device that measures and records data such as heart rate or temperature

tumor: an abnormal growth that can be dangerous to the body

vaccine: a substance containing dead or weak germs that is put in the body to train the immune system to fight that germ

virus: a germ that injects genes into healthy cells and causes diseases such as colds and flu

Learn More about the Future of Medicine

Books

Kenney, Karen Latchana. *What Makes Medical Technology Safer?* Minneapolis: Lerner Publications, 2016. Discover how medical technology keeps people healthy.

Senker, Cath. *The Science of Medical Technology*. New York: Franklin Watts, 2019. Learn about medical technology from vaccines to robot surgeons.

Silverman, Buffy. *Cutting-Edge Medicine*. Minneapolis: Lerner Publications, 2020. Dive deep into the world of medical breakthroughs.

Websites

Fact Monster: Medical Technology
https://www.factmonster.com/dk/encyclopedia/science/medical-technology
Uncover the importance of technology in modern medicine.

Technology and Medicine
http://broughttolife.sciencemuseum.org.uk/broughttolife/themes/technologies
Discover historic medical breakthroughs.

Time for Kids: Health
https://www.timeforkids.com/g34/sections/health-and-fitness/
Learn more about the latest medical news.

Index

Photo Acknowledgments

Image credits: Keith Lance/Getty Images, p. 4; Jose Luis Pelaez Inc/Getty Images, pp. 5, 11; Tassii/Getty Images, p. 6; AndreyPopov/Getty Images, p. 7; Isaac Lane Koval/Corbis/VCG/ Getty Images, p. 8; JUAN GARTNER/Getty Images, p. 9; vitapix/Getty Images, p. 10; CHRISTOPH BURGSTEDT/SCIENCE PHOTO LIBRARY/Getty Images, p. 12; Geng Ziye/Qianlong.com/Visual China Group/Getty Images, p. 13; traveler1116/Getty Images, p. 14; paulista/Shutterstock.com, p. 15; Sean Russell/Getty Images, p. 16; Manjurul/Getty Images, p. 17; Marcin Klapczynski/Getty Images, p. 18; piola666/Getty Images, p. 19; Ariel Skelley/Getty Images, p. 20; Andrew Brookes/ Getty Images, p. 21; metamorworks/Getty Images, p. 22; ER Productions Limited/Getty Images, p. 23; picture alliance/Getty Images, p. 24; monkeybusinessimages/Getty Images, p. 25; Picsfive/ Getty Images, p. 26; SCIEPRO/SCIENCE PHOTO LIBRARY/Getty Images, p. 27; Science Photo Library/Getty Images, p. 28; Tom Werner/Getty Images, p. 29.

Cover: Jackie Niam/Shutterstock.com.